Lawrence 1912

LAWRENCE 1912:
The Bread and Roses Strike

William Cahn

The Pilgrim Press ● New York

*Dedicated
to
Susan,
Kathe
and
Daniel.*

Aperture, Inc. as published in AMERICA AND LEWIS HINE Copywrite
© 1977. pp. 67 and 73.

The Bettmann Archive, Inc. pp. 37, 41, 42, 44, 77, 79, 83, 107, 159,
171, 183, and 231.

Brown Brothers p. 187.

Manchester (N.H.) Historic Association p. 239
Merrimac Valley Textile Museum pp. 39, 59, 75, and 81.
Museum of the City of New York, The Byron Collection p. 60

The Archives of Labor and Urban Affairs, Wayne State University pp.
41, 117, 137, 141, 147, 153, 161, 163, and 227

Jody Caravaglio photographs of Ralph Fasanella's Lawrence paintings
pp. 18 and 97.

The Rebel Girl p. 193

Red Cartoons, p. 62

Collection of Lee Baxandall p. 53

Second printing, January 1982

Library of Congress Cataloging in Publication Data

Cahn, William, 1912–
  Lawrence, 1912: the Bread and Roses Strike.

  A revision of the work published in 1954 under title:
Mill town.
  1. Lawrence Strike, 1912.   2. Textile workers—
Massachusetts—Lawrence—History.   3. Trade-unions—
Textile workers—Massachusetts—Lawrence—History.
4. Lawrence, Mass.—Social conditions. I. Title.
HD5325.T42 1912 L383 1980   331.89´2877´0097445
                                          80-10878

Editor's Note

William Cahn, noted author, first assembled a book on the Lawrence Strike of 1912 in the early 50's. Cahn was working on a revised version of the book when he died. The revision has been completed through the joint efforts of his friend Moe Foner with District 1199's Bread and Roses Project and The Pilgrim Press. Journalist Paul Cowan, a student of Lawrence and author of a moving description of the town for the Village Voice, has written a new introduction to the book, linking what happened to Lawrence in 1912 to what's happening in labor today.

History is often lost and regained. The city of Lawrence is an example. Lawrence is now in the process of regaining her history. Very few people discussed the strike until recent years, and even today, students and teachers alike are just beginning to study the rich and complex history of this community. Since the first publication of the book, the town has changed considerably, moving from the oddly silent place Cahn describes in the book's beginning to a more vibrant community attempting to grapple with its past, and use that past to build a strong and significant future.

ESTHER COHEN
THE PILGRIM PRESS

Preface

When the textile workers of Lawrence went on strike in 1912 for higher wages and better working conditions, they wrote one of the most stirring pages in the proud history of textile unionism in America—a history that leads directly to the present-day struggle of Southern textile workers to win justice.

Long before the Lawrence strike, textile workers banded together to protest their low wages and brutal conditions. And in the decades that followed the 1912 Lawrence strike, hundreds of thousands of wool, cotton, and silk mill workers throughout America rose up in revolt: in Paterson, New Jersey in 1913; in New Bedford, Massachusetts in 1928; in Gastonia, North Carolina in 1929, to name but a few. In 1934, 400,000 men and women responded to the call for an industry-wide strike. This was the largest walkout in American labor history.

But when clubs and bullets failed to defeat the workers' determination to join the Textile Workers Union of America in the 1930's and '40's the industry resorted to its ultimate weapon, moving South where unions were weak and wages low.

Since 1933, I have had the privilege of participating in the historic struggle of America's textile workers to organize. At no time in that period has there been a brighter outlook for textile unionism. Thanks to the courage and determination of textile workers throughout America and Canada, we're on the verge of a breakthrough in our campaign to organize the giant J. P. Stevens Company.

The Stevens workers have demonstrated that the spirit of Lawrence lives on. In 1912, textile workers in Lawrence demanded "Bread and Roses Too"—not just better wages, but a return of their human dignity. The 500,000 members of ACTWU have pledged themselves to struggle, until the dream of the Lawrence strikers of 1912 becomes a reality.

Sol Stetin
Senior Executive Vice President
ACTWU, AFL-CIO, CLC

Introduction

In 1912, it was possible for Americans to believe that economic democracy was a goal that could be achieved. In those days, the country was still in a state of flux, still trying to define itself. As part of the process, a panoply of political parties—the populists, the socialists, the single taxers—had elected Mayors, Congressmen and Senators who possessed an unflinching belief in the importance of redistributing income.

Of course, the labor movement was a lynchpin of that belief. And this book—the story of the great Lawrence textile strike of 1912—provides an important chapter in labor's saga.

For, that year, it seemed as if the tumultuous, two-month-long Lawrence strike (which spawned the lovely slogan "Bread and Roses, Too") might be the Appomattox of the battle for economic justice. The strike involved 20,000 people in a textile mill town of 90,000. It included immigrants from at least 30 different nations who spoke 45 different languages: Italians, Irish, Syrians, Armenians, Turks, Jews, Belgians, French-Canadians, Germans, Scandinavians all marched on the same picket lines. Some of those people—like Turks and Armenians, like Lithuanian Christians and Jews—had been bitter enemies in the old world. Now, in America, they had united to fight a common enemy—the poverty, the indignities, that came from working in the mills.

It all begun on January 12, 1912, when the mill owners, who had been ordered by the Massachusetts State Legislature to reduce the working week from 56 to 54 hours, forced the laborers to take a pay cut—*a pay cut from the $8.76 they made each week*. That day, thousands of workers surged through the city's biggest factory, the American Woolen Mill, sabatoging machinery to show their rage.

That night, Angelo Rocco, a 28-year-old Italian immigrant who had been a weaver in the mills, who was now attending Lawrence high school with the dream that some day he'd become a lawyer, telegraphed the International Workers of the World in New York to ask for help from some outside organizers. (Joseph Ettor of the IWW had already established contact with millhands in Lawrence.) Soon, an all-star cast of activists came to town. It included people like the great stump speaker Big Bill Haywood, the cool-headed Elizabeth Gurley Flynn, the poet and orator Arturo Giovannitti, Ettor, and a young socialist named Margaret Sanger whose advocacy of birth control methods would soon make her controversial and famous.

It was the first great industrial strike in America. Soon, it prompted nationally known journalists like Lincoln Steffens and Ray Stannard Baker to come to Lawrence and investigate working conditions in the mills, living conditions in the tenaments.

Meanwhile, the Yankee aristocracy which ran the mills was enraged at the immigrants who had overcome the barriers of language and culture to fight together for social justice. Their organ, *New England Magazine*, warned its readers that the town was the scene of "a wage war which will spread throughout the country. The conditions which exist [in Lawrence] are largely the result of our immigration laws. For years, the offscourings of Southern Europe have been pouring into the city and working for wages Americans could not compete with. They will not be assimilated [and] have no sympathy for our institutions."

The readers of *New England Magazine* were right to be worried. For the strikers won the first, stunning triumph in American industrial history. And the truth was that many of the workers, whom their bosses saw as "offscourings," had received excellent academic and political educations through their affiliations with socialist parties back in Europe. They knew the value of careful strategic planning, of effective nationwide publicity campaigns, of soup kitchens for hungry workers, of non-violent tactics like mobile picket lines. They were more skilled than their adversaries. Their ingenuity caused the mill owners to overreact.

Their most effective strategy was the children's exodus from Lawrence. The strike took place in January and February, bitterly cold months, and the organizers decided to find secure housing outside town for some of the activists' offspring. It was not only a thoughtful humanitarian measure; it was also an immensely effective public relations technique.

In Lawrence, the kids and their parents would go to the railroad station, bearing signs with slogans like "We Shall Never Forget Our Exile," and board trains for New York or Providence or Philadelphia. Wherever they went, they got a friendly reception in the press. They were always met by large groups of supporters who sometimes placed them in the forefront of torchlight parades. Reporters invariably questioned the children about working conditions in the mills. Soon, for much of the nation, the Lawrence mills were a symbol of shame.

The mill owners and the city government decided to use intimidation as the main weapon in their counter-offensive. One February morning they dispatched a squadron of policemen to the railroad station. The police surrounded a train bound for Philadelphia and beat up some of the children—and their parents—as they attempted to board it.

That attack became a nationwide scandal. Shortly after it, Margaret Sanger, always a shrewd strategist, arranged for about 20 strikers and their children to testify before the House Committee on Rules in Washington.

Camella Teoli, the daughter of Italian immigrants, once a millhand, was the strikers' most effective witness. For her short story condensed all the exploitation, all the random dangers, that had triggered the strike in the first place.

"I used to go to school," the girl began, "and then a man [a factory agent] came up to my house and asked my father why I didn't go to work. So my father says 'I don't know whether she is 13 or 14.' [Under child labor laws, 14 was the minimum working age.] So the man said 'you give me $4 and I will make papers come from the old country which say she is 14.' So my father gave him the $4, and in one month came the papers that I was 14."

Two weeks after she'd started work at the Washington Mills, Camella Teoli was scalped: her hair got caught in a machine for twisting cotton. She was hospitalized for the next seven months. The company paid her doctors' bills, but not her lost wages. Of course, no one tried to restore the educational possibilities she'd lost when the factory agent first came to her door.

Camella Teoli's story became front page news all over America—especially because Mrs. William Howard Taft, the President's wife, was in the audience the day the immigrant child told her story to the House Committee on Rules. The details Camella described were grisly enough to help prompt a government investigation of working conditions throughout America. And the publicity helped the strikers win their unprecedented victory: a 10 percent pay hike, the right to overtime pay, and amnesty from arrest.

In Lawrence, though, the successful strike was followed by a period of intense reaction, which affected Camella Teoli among others.

The Protestant mill owners, and the Irish and Italian Catholic churches, which were immensely powerful in those days, sought to brand the most visible strikers as radicals and unsavory immigrants. They were helped by some of the insurgents' tactical mistakes. For example, at a rally in September, 1912—six months after the strike ended—a small group of people (some old-timers say Poles, others say Italian anarchists) carried a banner which read "No God, No Master." Soon afterwards—on Columbus Day, 1912—a priest named Father James O'Reilly persuaded 50,000 people to demonstrate visible opposition to that kind of atheistic defiance by attending a "For God, For Country" parade. Soon the insurgents, not the working conditions in the mills, became the main issue in Lawrence.

Many of the activists grew bitter—or scared. Some of the 1912 generation of strikers grew discouraged when the IWW organizers left town to fight their next labor war. Others developed the bleak certainty that most workers had become passive—that they cared more about job security than about repeated fights for economic justice. Others were intimidated by the post-World War I Palmer Raids, where thousands of foreign-born radicals were rounded up and hundreds were deported. The Italians particularly, saw the execution of Sacco and Vanzetti as an example of what could happen to any immigrant who remained committed to fighting for sweeping political change.

Nevertheless, Lawrence remained a pro-union town. Throughout the 1930's and 40's the Textile Clothing Workers Union of America waged successful organizing drives. In a way, those drives threatened the mill owners as much as the 1912 strike had. For the workers kept winning higher wages.

So, soon most textile mills moved South, to Georgia and the Carolinas, where they could increase their profits by hiring cheap, non-union labor. Lawrence became a desolate place, forgotten by a nation that had once heralded it as a symbol of social change. The relatively few people who remembered the 1912 strike were reluctant to discuss it, for fear that they would once again be branded as subversives. For decades, the town's proud past was a buried memory. It took courage simply to remember.

I saw that in February, 1976, when I decided to search for Camella Teoli and write about her in the Village Voice. A cousin of hers—whose name I found in a phone book—told me she'd died a few years earlier. But, he added, for a decade before that she had lived with a daughter whom I'll call Mathilda, a store manager who was the wife of a butcher. Mathilda had a home in a nearby suburb. I called her at 10 o'clock one night.

At first she thought I was a crank—a late night voice raving incomprehensibly about something that had happened 64 years ago. Then I mentioned Camella Teoli's scalping. It was as if I'd unlocked a magic box of trust: furnished proof that there was some sort of link between Camella Teoli and me. For the accident at the Washington Mills had left Camella Teoli with a permanent scar—a bald spot towards the back of her head that was six inches in diameter. Practically every day of her life, Mathilda had combed her mother's hair into a bun that disguised the spot.

Suddenly, she seemed eager to see me. She suggested that we have breakfast at a shopping mall the next morning.

As soon as we met I realized why my unexpected phone call had been so very confusing. Without much pause for formalities I began to ask about the 1912 strike. But Mathilda knew nothing at all about Camella Teoli's political past—nothing abut her trip to Washington, nothing about Mrs. William Howard Taft's presence, nothing about the sensational impact her mother had made on the nation's conscience. The Camella Teoli her children knew was just a mill hand with an odd bald spot on her head, a sweet, silent lady who bought and cooked the traditional eels on Christmas Eve, who rarely missed a Sunday mass. She'd been swept up in the immigrants' reluctance to discuss their heroic past. She had never once mentioned the trip to Washington, which must have been the proudest moment of her life.

That day in Lawrence, I was carrying two books which contained transcripts of Camella Teoli's testimony. Standing in that huge parking lot, she read her mother's account of the old days in the Washington mills. I drove her to the Lawrence library, where there was a two-volume record of the 1912 hearing. She read her mother's testimony, enraptured. "Now I have a past," she said. "Now my son has a history."

Like her, most of the former strikers I met in 1976 were loathe to discuss the event. And the few who did were afraid to let me quote them by name. Their comments suggested that Camella Teoli had remained silent in order to protect herself—and her young—from reprisals.

Most of the strike leaflets had been printed at an Italian immigrant's print shop. During the post World War I Palmer Raids—where tens of thousands of radicals were arrested and thousands of immigrants were deported—government agents had called the printer an "undesirable alien." A friend had told him he might be deported. In his world, it was common to spend time away from one's family, away from one's work, in hiding.

He did that for a spell. In 1976 his son, still worried, insisted on concealing his name for fear that his business would be boycotted.

One day I tried to talk with one of the "children" who had gone into exile during the strike—a city employee who spent most of his time playing the card game *briscola* with other older men. He didn't want to retire, so he needed the city's good will to keep his job. He had vivid memories of his trip away from Lawrence and an enduring respect for the strike and the strike leaders. But he didn't want to discuss the past. "You have to understand," he said. "I'm a very popular kid around here. I don't want to go around giving away the city's secrets."

In those years, even the dream of economic democracy seemed distant indeed.

But what if Lawrence hadn't been enveloped in an atmosphere of intimidation? What if children like Camella Teoli had been able to grow up in the political world that seemed so promising in 1912? She—and dozens like her—would have been able to take advantage of the Italian culture that strike leaders like Joseph Ettor and Arturo Giovannitti were so eager to transmit—to retain Italian as a language so that they'd have access to writers like Dante, composers like Verdi, political thinkers like Gramsci—to feel that they weren't illiterate peasants but heirs to a culture that was even finer than that of the Yankees who defined them as brutes.

When you realize that most of the people whose pictures you see in this book would have had access to similar cultures, then Mathilda's spontaneous exclamation in the Lawrence library— "Now I have a past, now my son has a history"—becomes as much a lament as a cry of joy.

The situation has improved in the last four years.

Most people complain that the late 1970's was a time of reaction in America. But, during that period, mill towns in general, and Lawrence in particular, held promises of new progress. Because of the Amalgamated Clothing and Textile Workers' Union campaign against J. P. Stevens, America's second largest textile company, the North Carolina and Georgia towns to which the mill owners had fled were no longer safe havens. A new, progressive city government in Lawrence encouraged the ex-strikers who'd been silent for decades to speak out. The vein of radical history—and immigrant history—which had been hidden for so long can now be tapped.

Plainly, the union drive that is spreading through the 83 J. P. Stevens factories in the South can become a second Lawrence. For there, too, people who've been enemies for centuries are beginning to band together against a common economic enemy. It's clear that most Stevens managers chose to move South because they assumed that black and white employees would never form an alliance—and because they assumed that few people of either race would gamble the wages they were earning in the dangerous struggle for a union. But they were wrong—in great part because the danger of brown lung, which comes from inhaling cotton dust, is at least as great a danger as machine-related injuries were in Camella Teoli's day. Unions—which mean workers' safety committees—can literally mean the difference between life and death.

Louis Harell is a modern-day Camella Teoli, who has died of cancer since he was interviewed by Mimi Conway for her powerful book *Rise Gonna Rise*. Listen to him describe the ailment the union is trying to combat.

"My chest feels like its gonna bust. And you know how your arm feels when they take your blood pressure? Well, mine feels exactly like that.

"You know, until I got that hospital bed over yonder, I used to just go to sleep sitting in my chair, when I got so bad I couldn't lie down.

"The first time I started having lung trouble other than for shortness of breath on a bad day was about seven or eight years ago. Then every time I caught a cold or bronchitis I couldn't get no breath. Then I started to have heart trouble. Then they said I was having a breathing problem and that's what was giving me the heart.

"The mostest thing that bothers me is walking. I've got where I can't walk far. Yesterday I walked from the parking lot to my job and I had to halt. . . . "

Geographically, the Stevens struggle is far more complex than the campaign in Lawrence was. For the 83 plants are scattered throughout three states, and they employ 44,000 people. In the past seven years six of those plants have won the right to have union bargaining agents, either through elections or through court orders. In October, 1979, the union won a major election at the Stevens plant in High Point, North Carolina—a victory which, organizers hope, will speed the entire campaign.

It will be a time consuming battle, though—as was Cesar Chavez' fight to organize the Farmworkers. It can't be dramatized by a single episode, like the childrens' exile in Lawrence. It involves town-by-town organizing, a nationwide boycott of J. P. Stevens products, and a complex series of court cases to establish—quite simply—the right to campaign for a union in a Southern mill. It will probably end when J. P. Stevens executives decide that the company is too economically and politically embattled to keep fighting.

Right now, the campaign is an important reminder that the labor union is reviving. And, in this time of ethnic tension, it is an important reminder that when people share a common need, they don't decide integration: they display it.

In Lawrence, in 1977, a new, young Mayor, Lawrence LeFebre, brought an administration of progressive people into the City Hall. Unlike their predecessors, many of whom were wedded to Father O'Reilly's dour view of the 1912 strike, they were open-minded people who were eager to reinterpret the city's history. In 1978, Ralph Fassenella's pro-strike paintings—some of which are contained in this book—were exhibited in the Lawrence library. That, in itself, would have been impossible just two years earlier. The city officials heralded the show, and thousands of adults and school children came to see it. The city was recovering some pride in its buried past.

That pride intensified over the next year. When I went to Lawrence to research this introduction I was asked to give speeches about the strike in grade schools and in high schools, where it had rarely been mentioned in 1976. Teachers were developing oral history programs, where students would talk with older people, especially their own grandparents, about the mill town's history, and about its extraordinary labor movement. Like Fassanella, I went on Louis Marcelle's Hot Line, a popular noon-time talk show. Mayor LeFebre called up and encouraged everyone who remembered the strike to talk with me and Ignatius Piscitello, the head of the Lawrence Historical Preservation Society. Dozens did. Now most were proud to give their names. On the show, there was the inevitable debate over Father O'Reilly—some callers thought he was right, that the IWW had led local people down the path of godless Communism, others disagreed—but at last the festering argument was aired publically.

Right now, almost all of Lawrence's streets bear old New England Yankee names—there's an Andover Street, for example, a Lawrence Street, a Lowell Street, an Essex Street. In other words, there is no recognition, amid all those symbols, that the peaceful 1850's world out of which the town was created had ever been altered.

Now, though, Mayor LeFebre plans to name one of the streets in town after Camella Teoli and perhaps, to start a labor museum as two ways of reasserting the value of the textile strike.

For, as people in Lawrence are beginning to insist, the mill town has a great deal to share with the rest of America—as the Southern towns in the J. P. Stevens campaign will one day. At a time when America is becoming increasingly polarized, by race and by ethnic groups, the strike shows that people can overcome age-old cultural differences if they share a common goal. It shows that bosses (those who own textile mills and those who own multi-national corporations) are not all powerful. Will power and sophisticated tactics can defeat them. Finally, it shows that heroic protest movements mustn't be relegated to the past, for they contain legacies of memory, of hope, of idealism, that can enrich everyone whose lives have been touched by their gains. Movements like the one this book depicts intertwine with the present.

Taken together, the new political activities in the mill towns—the J. P. Stevens campaign and Lawrence's renewal of self-esteem—are signs that in the 1980's, as in 1912, it may be possible for America to believe, once again, that economic justice is a goal that can be achieved.

PAUL COWAN

Contents

This is the tale of a city . . .
of its people . . .
and of their history . . .

Our story starts long ago—around 1840—when a man by the name of Daniel Saunders had an idea.

Secretly he bought up land on both sides of the Merrimac River just north of Lowell. And secretly he met with a group of Boston financiers interested in investing capital where it would yield a profitable return. Especially did Saunders interest members of the wealthy Lawrence family. . . .

Abbott Lawrence

The Lawrence brothers—Samuel, Abbott and Amos—had one idea in common: to make money.

"If you are troubled with the belief that I am growing too rich," Abbott Lawrence told an acquaintance, *"there is one thing you may as well understand: I know how to make money."*

Said his brother, Amos, *"We have some ambitions to buy cheap and sell . . . high."*

And so Daniel Saunders interested the Lawrence brothers in investing in the building of a city. . . .

24

VIEW OF THE CITY OF LAWRENCE MASS.
DEDICATED TO
SAMUEL LAWRENCE ESQUIRE.

The Lawrence brothers put $100,000 into founding the city which was to bear their name. In a few years a great dam was built across the Merrimac River to supply power for the running of factories. This was Daniel Saunders' dream.

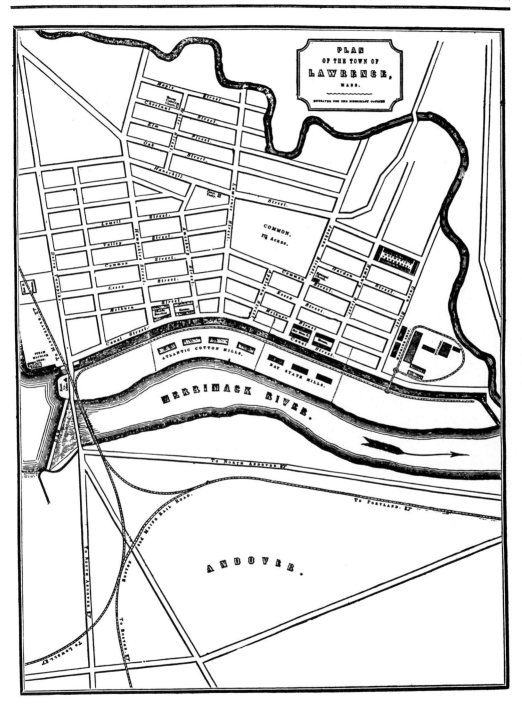

Soon after, the first textile mill was built. . . .

The first canals—to bring water power right to the mill gates—were dug. . . .

The machinery came . . .

. . . and the city grew. . . .

But what of the *people* for the new city?

Those were the days before big, mass-production factories. Much of the work—especially in making cloth—was done in the home.

The new factories had to send wagons into the countryside to recruit "rosy-cheeked maidens" to work in the city mills. In time the recruiting wagons came to be known as *"slavers."*

TIME TABLE
OF THE
COCHECO MILLS.
MARCH, 1856.

Arranged to make the working hours throughout the year average 11 hours per day.

From March 1st to October 31st, inclusive.

Commence Work at 6.30 A. M. Leave off Work at 6.30 P. M., except on Saturday Evenings. Breakfast at 6 A. M. Dinner 12 M. Commence work after dinner 12.45 P. M.

From November 1st to February 28th, inclusive.

Commence Work at 7 A. M. Leave off Work at 7 P. M., except on Saturday Evenings. Breakfast at 6.30 A. M. Dinner 12.30 P. M. Commence work after dinner 1.15 P. M.

BELLS.

From March 1st to October 31st, inclusive.

MORNING BELLS.		DINNER BELLS.	
First Bell, 4.30 A. M.	Second Bell, 5.30 A. M.	Ring Out,	12 M
Third Bell, 6.20 "		Ring In,	12.45 P. M

From November 1st to February 28th, inclusive.

| First Bell, 5.00 A. M. | Second Bell, 6.00 A. M. | Ring Out, | 12.30 P. M |
| Third Bell, 6.50 " | | Ring In, | 1.15 " |

SATURDAY EVENING BELLS.

During the month of March, Ring out at 5.30, and April, May, June, July and August, 6.30 P. M.
The remaining Saturdays in the year, as follows.

September.		November.		January.	
First Saturday,	6.00 P. M	First Saturday,	4.23 P. M	First Saturday,	4.11 P. M
Second "	5.55 "	Second "	4.14 "	Second "	4.18 "
Third "	5.42 "	Third "	4.07 "	Third "	4.27 "
Fourth "	5.30 "	Fourth "	4.01 "	Fourth "	4.35 "
Fifth "	5.17 "				

October.		December.		February.	
		First Saturday,	3.50 P. M	First Saturday,	4.45 P. M
First Saturday,	5.05 P. M	Second "	3.58 "	Second "	4.55 "
Second "	4.54 "	Third "	3.58 "	Third "	5.03 "
Third "	4.43 "	Fourth "	4.01 "	Fourth "	5.12 "
Fourth "	4.32 "	Fifth "	4.05 "		

Yard Gates will be opened when the Bell for commencing work begins to ring, and closed when it stops tolling. Ringing in Bells, will ring 5 minutes, pause 2, and toll 3 minutes, when they will not be in. Mill Gates will be hoisted when the last Bell begins to ring.

Workers in the new plants were mostly women. Hours were from 6 A.M. to 10 P.M., six days a week. Wages averaged about $1.50 for such a period.

One poet of the era wrote:
> "Oh! Isn't it a pity
> That such a pretty girl as I
> Should be sent to the factory
> To pine away and die."

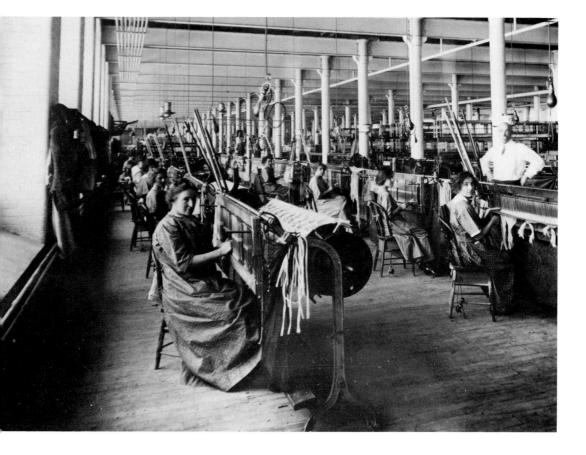

Children, too, were sent into the factories as a means—so the mill owners put it—*"to keep them from mischief."*

Sarah N. Cleghorn wrote:
> *The golf links lie so near the mill*
> *That almost every day*
> *The laboring children can look out*
> *And see the men at play.*

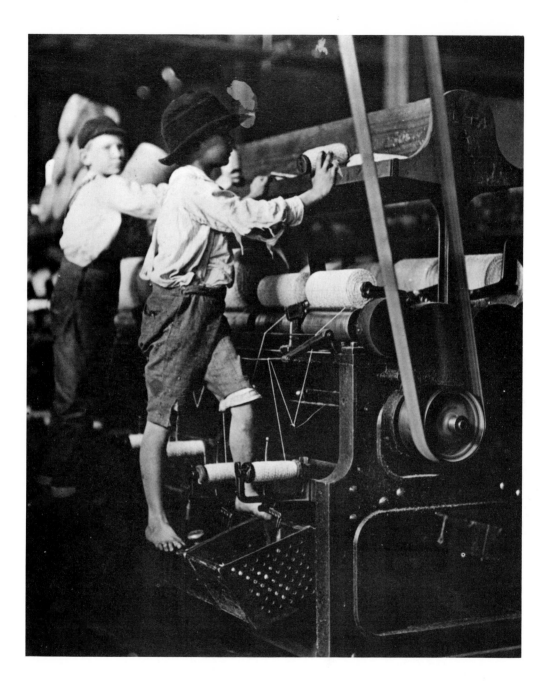

Children, even as young as five years, worked in the mills, many
of them 14 hours a day, six days a week! Punishments were
common as the foreman or "overseer" system came into being.

"They have to be constantly watched," said the employers'
newspaper, *Textile World,"* or they will go from bad to worse in order
to make more time for play."*

There was danger in the newly built mills—for men, women and children.

One cotton plant in Lawrence—the Pemberton mill—was constructed too rapidly. On January 10, 1860, the entire factory collapsed, burying 670 workers—including women and children—in the ruins.

Night fell. Fire broke out. Hundreds were killed and additional hundreds were seriously injured. An investigation concluded that "defective pillars were . . . the primary cause of the disaster."

AN

AUTHENTIC HISTORY

OF THE

LAWRENCE CALAMITY

EMBRACING A

DESCRIPTION OF THE PEMBERTON MILL,

A DETAILED ACCOUNT OF THE CATASTROPHE,

A CHAPTER OF THRILLING INCIDENTS,

LIST OF CONTRIBUTIONS TO THE RELIEF FUND, NAMES OF THE KILLED AND WOUNDED,

ABSTRACTS OF SERMONS ON THE SUBJECT,

REPORT OF THE CORONER'S INQUEST, &c.

BOSTON:
JOHN J. DYER & CO., 35 SCHOOL STREET,
1860.

mourners in words of consolation, and in the prayer which followed, invoked the blessing of the Almighty upon the widow and the fatherless children of the deceased.

LIST OF THE DEAD AND INJURED.

The following list of the dead, badly injured, slightly injured, and missing or unidentified, has been officially revised and corrected, and is believed to be accurate. It was compiled by Hon. John R. Rollins, Ex-Mayor. It will be seen that the total number of dead and missing, is ninety; of this number, seventy-six bodies have been recovered and recognized, thirteen are yet unrecognized, leaving but one missing.

Dead—Total, 76.

Mary Ann Bannon,
Bridget Bronder,
William Jordan,
Joanna Cronan,
Irene Crosby,
Hannah Shea,
Margaret Sullivan,
Dennis Leonard,
Wm. Metcalf,
John C. Dearborn,
Peter Callahan,
Bernard Hollifield,
Margaret Hamilton,
Ellen Colbert,
Mary Griffin,
Catherine Hannon,
Michael O'Brien,
Margaret Foley,
Mary Culloten,
Kate Conners,
Margaret Fallon,
Joanna Hurley,
Mary Howard,
Martin Hughes,
Margaret Corcoran,
Bridget Crosby,
Catherine Kelleher,
Eliza Orr,
Julia Roberts,
Bridget Ryan,
Wm. Kane,
Wm. Adolph,
Elizabeth R. Kimball,
Richard Lunney,
Ann Sullivan,
Mary Jewett,
Richard Midgely,
Ellen Hickey,

Lizzie Towne,
Ellen Mahoney,
Orin C. Nash,
Samuel Rolfe,
Bridget Loughrey,
Morris C. Palmer,
Matthew C. Ryan,
Hannah Mulinex,
Mary McCann,
Catherine Cooney,
Ellen Sullivan,
Ellen Dinneen,
Mary Dooley,
James Harty,
James Hartigan,
Catherine O'Brien,
Mary Nice,
Mary Murphy,
Catherine Sweeny,
Margaret Coleman,
Mary Barrett,
Elizabeth Dunn,
Catherine Harrigan,
Augusta Ashworth,
Ellen Ahern,
Patrick Connor,
Lafayette F. Branch,
Ellen Conners,
Ellen Roach,
Margaret Turnor,
Mary Burke,
Bridget Gallan,
Lorinda Gilson,
Jane Thomas,
Katy Clarke,
John Hughes,
Maggie J. Smith,
Celia A. Stevens.

Missing or Unidentified.—Total, 14.

Bridget Kelly,
John McNab,
Asenath S. Martin,
Sarah Lyons,
Ellen Linkinson,
Margaret Donnelly,
Eliza Wahiggan,

Joseph Baily,
Henry Harrigan,
Dora Harold,
Mary Ryan.
Jeremiah Ahern,
Ellen Robinson,
Lizzie A. Flint.

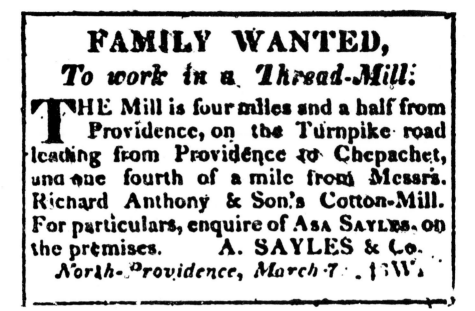

FAMILY WANTED,

To work in a Thread-Mill:

THE Mill is four miles and a half from Providence, on the Turnpike road leading from Providence to Chepachet, und one fourth of a mile from Messrs. Richard Anthony & Son's Cotton-Mill. For particulars, enquire of Asa Sayles, on the premises.   A. SAYLES & Co.

North-Providence, March 7. 18W.

The mill owners borrowed from the methods of Samuel Slater—father of the American factory system. It was Slater also who introduced in this country the idea of hiring complete families in the shop.

To justify low wage scales, the mill owners spread the idea that *"the higher the wages, the more leisure, the more idleness."*

"I regard my work people," said one mill owner, *"just as I regard my machinery."*

50

Samuel Slater, who is credited with establishing "speed-up" methods of factory production in this country.

Unions were the answer of many working people to increasing exploitation in the mills and factories. And although employers called labor organizations "conspiracies," they continued to attract increasing membership.

Robert Koehler, "The Strike" 1886

By the turn of the century a young and vigorous labor movement—the American Federation of Labor—demanded and won an eight-hour day for many thousands of craft workers. Under the leadership of Samuel Gompers labor moved forward with its slogan: *"Eight hours for work, eight hours for rest, eight hours for what we will."*

THE FEDERATION OF LABOR

TRADES UNIONISTS FORM A NEW ORGANIZATION.

THE KNIGHTS OF LABOR IGNORED AND A CONSTITUTION FOR THE NEW BODY ADOPTED—OFFICERS ELECTED.

COLUMBUS, Ohio, Dec. 11.—It will doubtless prove a trifle galling to Terence Vincent Powderly and his old Executive Board to learn that the trades unionists, who have been in session here for the best part of ... ed as President of their ... American Federation ... pers, the man he ... circular that wa... The fact that Mr. ... opposition may ... estimation in wh... ists. The latter... own way. They ... position, in the ... lieutenants wit... their powers a... day between ... vals. The n... the Knights ... existence long ... begins life with... There is reason ... will join the f... held. Its prim... bers every tra... and some of ... object abo... Heret... enroll... gla...

Eight Hours for Work,
Eight Hours for Recreation,
Eight Hours for Sleep.

But businessmen were active too—uniting their forces . . . forming combinations . . . gobbling up smaller competitors . . . making vast profits. . . .

Huge factories began to spring up. In Lawrence, for example, such plants were constructed as the Pacific mill, the Ayer mill, the Arlington mill.

Care was taken to keep the city a one-industry town. There would be no competitive bidding for labor—to send wage levels up.

Total Length over 1900 feet. Width 125 feet Total floor space 1,300,000 sq. ft. Cost $3,500,000 Employees 5,000

In 1905 the gigantic Wood mill, named after William M. Wood, president of the American Woolen Co., was built in Lawrence. It was the largest cloth-producing factory in the world.

This giant of Lawrence was a mighty U-shaped building, more than a third of a mile long, 30 acres all under one roof. The eye could not take it all in at one glance.

When hiring was at its peak, almost 10,000 workers were employed here.

At this time the American Woolen Co. was growing from one mill to more than 27 mills. *The New York Times* referred to the company as *"The $65,000,000 wool trust."*

Horseback Dinner at Sherry's, 1903

On the national scene, in the steel, mining, electrical as well as textile industries, business was combining into gigantic monopolies or "trusts."

"For years capital has been organized, bold, unscrupulous, law-defying," a United States Senator told the 42nd Congress, *"unblushingly purchasing judges and legislatures."*

Wall Street in New York City became the symbol of the concentration of great wealth in the hands of a few.

60

Wall Street—1912

● *"I am not in Wall Street for my health,"* stated J. P. Morgan.

The financiers of the day did not then feel it necessary to disguise their aims.

● *"We accept and welcome . . . the concentration of business in the hands of the few,"* asserted Andrew Carnegie.

● *"The public be damned,"* said William Vanderbilt.

But conditions in the shops were growing worse. The "rosy-cheeked" maidens who had flocked to the new factories were leaving.

And those that had to remain began to listen more and more seriously to talk about "organization" and "unions." Working people found they had common problems and needed to unite, as one spokesman said: *"not as Germans, Irishmen or Americans, not as Whigs or Democrats . . . unite and organize as workers."*

Working people shown leaving Lawrence mills at end of their 13-hour work day. The picture, entitled "Bell Time," is by the noted American artist Winslow Homer.

Industry needed more workers. Needed them urgently. So postcards and posters were dispatched to nations overseas to attract people to our shores.

Posters showed a working man leaving a factory in Lawrence, Mass. He carried a suitcase full of gold. And in the distance was the bank to which he was taking it.

Thousands risked the long trip to come to the new land of opportunity. . . .

The immigrants came. Thousands entered the mills of Lawrence. The city became a center for a score of nationalities, eager to work, to earn, to raise their families in this new land. . . .

But they soon found all was not the way the posters had pictured
it.

A survey of industrial cities of 1909 stated that an average
family *"cannot live and maintain efficiency . . . for less than $900 a
year."*

Yet Lawrence workers were paid far less. In addition, the fear
of unemployment hung over the head of almost every worker.

*"Husky, able-bodied men would steal by the watchmen and get into
the mill,"* an article in the *American Magazine* stated in regard to
Lawrence conditions, *"and then beg . . . for a job where they could
make any wages at all. There are many able-bodied men today in the
Lawrence mills doing children's jobs, taking children's places and
receiving the pitiful children's wages. . . . "*

Housing conditions were miserable. "Workers were forced to live," according to the *New York Times,* "in tenements owned by the American Woolen Co. for which they paid high rents."

The housing situation was, as the White Survey described it: *"darkness and dampness and dirt; dirt and discomfort and disease; death."*

Discrimination in the mills was widespread.

One nationality was pitted against another to keep workers disunited. For example, in one department of the American Woolen Co., the Polish workers were threatened with replacement by Italians unless they worked faster.

So few Negro workers were hired that there were only 265 families living in the entire city, according to a Government survey.

Children often had to forego their schooling and enter the plants to help their families survive. . . .

"*A considerable number of the boys and girls die within the first two or three years after beginning work,*" stated Dr. Elizabeth Shapleigh of Lawrence. "*Thirty-six out of every 100 of all men and women who work in the mill die before or by the time they are 25 years of age.*"

Hours of work were long, averaging 60 a week. Working conditions, according to Prof. Harry F. Ward of the Boston University School of Theology, *"were unbearable."*

Women were encouraged to enter the mills . . . to work at wages considerably lower than men. *"They have forced our wives to the mills to work alongside of us,"* the workers were to state later, *"not that their wages be leveled up to men, but that the men be forced to compete with women."*

In addition, there were other problems. As one "heartbroken mother" wrote a Congressman: *"Please investigate the social conditions. . . . See if there are girls employed that have to cater to the passions of the boss to hold their positions."*

A survey made in Lawrence in 1911 showed "serious contamination" of the city's milk supply.

"There is little or no supervision or inspection from the time it is produced until it is consumed," said the White Report. "The City has been giving practically no attention to the milk supply. . . . "

In regard to sewage disposal, the Report stated: "There seems to be no limitations in the use of (the) river for sewage purposes . . . a greater menace to good health than has heretofore been understood."

Despite this, the survey found, the Lawrence Board of Health placed *"foremost in its deliberations the subject of licenses for stables."*

WARNING !

Do not drink this canal water — it will make you sick.

AVIS !

Il est défendu de faire usage de l'eau du canal pour boire — elle pourrait vous rendre malade.

OSTRZEŻENIE!

Nie pijaj wody z kanalu tego, bo zachorujesz.

ACAUTELEM-SE!

Nao bebam a agua do Canal. Fas-te doente.

ΠΡΟΣΟΧΗ

ΜΗ ΠΙΝΕΤΕ ΝΕΡΟ ΑΠΟ ΤΟ ΚΑΝΑΛΙ: Θ' ΑΡΡΩΣΤΗΣΕΤΕ.

E. H. WALKER, Agent

The American Federation of Labor, under the leadership of Gompers, did much to better the conditions of working people, especially skilled workers in the craft fields. But the great mass of working people in the factories and mills—for the most part unskilled and poorly paid—were not organized.

John Golden became president of the United Textile Workers, AFL, the largest organization of textile workers of the time. However, Golden was slow to organize the industrial workers. In 1912, for example, there were only 208 AFL textile workers in the entire city of Lawrence.

82

Labor leaders, such as Bill Haywood, head of the Western Federation of Miners, gave voice to the people's need for curbing the mighty corporations . . . for unionism . . . for *industrial unionism.* . . .

Mother Jones, beloved champion of mine workers for three-quarters of a century, spoke out against child labor: *"Some day the workers will take possession of your city hall,"* she warned the employers, *"and when we do, no child will be sacrificed on the altar of profit."*

84

Mrs. Mary (Mother) Jones

Other labor leaders were also coming forward. Eugene V. Debs, founder of the Brotherhood of Railroad Trainmen and a fighting advocate of industrial unionism, stated: *"I would encourage industrial independent organization especially among the millions who have not been organized at all. . . .*

"The capitalists refer to you as mill hands," Debs continued, *"farm hands, factory hands . . . hands . . . hands . . . hands . . . a capitalist would feel insulted if you called him a hand . . . he's a head. The trouble is he owns your head and your hands!"*

86

Eugene V. Debs

But the forces speaking out for company interests were powerful. There was young Theodore Roosevelt, who said: *"The worst foe of the poor man is the labor leader . . . who tries to teach him he is a victim of conspiracy and injustice."*

And Judge Elbert H. Gary, chairman of the U.S. Steel Co., who stated at a Waldorf-Astoria banquet of big financiers in New York:

"Certain labor agitators . . . have made most desperate efforts . . . to incite trouble, to bring about a feeling of discontent and to cause rupture between the employers of labor and the employees."

● *"I never had time to count how many automobiles I own,"* stated William M. Wood.

In Lawrence, fearful of further wage cuts as a result of a pending reduction in working hours, a committee of working people from the American Woolen Co., Wood mill, sought to see Mr. Wood.

They were told to write him at the Boston office.

The group carefully addressed a special delivery letter to him, stating that conditions were unbearable.

There was no answer.

Mr. Wood's garage

Typical worker's home

These were the conditions that faced the 35,000 mill workers of Lawrence on the eve of 1912 just as the Massachusetts state legislature—responding in a small way to public pressure—passed a law reducing hours for women and minors from 56 to 54 a week.

Said William M. Wood for the mill owners: *"To pay for 54 hours' work the wages of 56 would be equivalent to an increase in wages, and that the mills cannot afford to pay."*

RE. —Report for ... ending Aug. 31 1911, in V. 93, p. ... showed net profits over expenses and interest, $331,803; div. on common (4%), $160,000; div. on pref., $140,000; bal., sur., $31,803. Pres., R. W. Nelson, 300 Communipaw Ave., Jersey City.—(V. 93, p. **1104**.)

AMERICAN WINDOW GLASS MACHINE CO.—See page 182 to 185.

AMERICAN WOOLEN CO.—ORGANIZATION.—Incorporated March 29 1899 under laws of N. J. as a consolidation of the Washington Mills, Lawrence, Mass.; National Providence Mills, Providence, R. I., &c.; see V. 68, p. 472; see also p. 617; V. 69, p. 77; V. 73, p. 446; V. 71, p. 545. List of properties, V. 78, p. 1118; V. 90, p. 622; V. 91, p. 1162; V. 71, p. 1316.

Owned 1909 775 sets of cards, 8,495 looms, 325 combs, 6,000,000 spindles.

The Wood Worsted Mill Corporation, which was merged in Sept. 1910, owned a large mill at South Lawrence, Mass., for the manufacture of yarns and men's wear fabrics; its $3,500,000 notes, guar. p. & i., $500,000 paid Mch. 1910, $1,500,000 Sept. 1910 and remainder, $1,000,000, Mch. 1911. V. 81, p. 900, 842; V. 84, p. 1054; V. 86, p. 599; V. 90, p. 622; V. 91, p. 522, 1162.

The Ayer Mills, whose stock is owned, built a yarn mill at South Lawrence, Mass.; commenced operation in July 1910. The $2,000,000 4½% notes of 1910 mature $500,000 each Mch. 1 1913 and 1914 and $1,000,000 Mch. 1 1915, and the $2,000,000 4½% notes of 1911 (issued to refund the $2,000,-000 due June 1911) $1,000,000 each Mch. 1 1915 and 1917. V. 88, p. 508; V. 90, p. 622, 701; V. 92, p. 1312.

STOCK.—In 1909 issued $5,000,000 pref. V. 88, p. 1622; V. 89, p. 227. Dividends on pref. July 1899 to Jan. 1912 both incl., 7% per an.(Q.J.15).

The stockholders voted April 28 1911 to reduce the common stock from $30,000,000 to $20,000,000 by canceling $_____,900 stock never issued and also $9,501,100 stock bought in by the company.

EARNINGS.—Status Oct. 1911, V. 93, p. 1193. Report for year 1910 in V. 92, p. 657, showed: Net profits, $3,995,310; pref. divs. (7%), $2,800,-000; depreciation, $538,664; surplus, $656,646; total surplus, $11,121,455.

DIRECTORS.—Wm. M. Wood (Pres.), Frederick Ayer, John Hogg, F. W. Kittredge, J. C. Woodhull, G. E. Bullard, Andrew G. Pierce Jr., Geo. L. Shepley and Chas. H. Tenney; Sec. and Treas., W. H. Dwelly Jr.; Asst. Treas., W. A. Currier; Asst. Sec., Frederic G. Sherman. Office, Shawmut Bank Bldg., Boston, Mass.—(V. 92, p. 1312; V. 93, p. 732, 1193.)

AMERICAN WRITING PAPER CO.—ORGANIZATION.—Incorpor-
consolidati... ... ... ing ...

"Strike!"

On January 12, 1912, one of the greatest mass protests in American history took place. . . .

Police in
From
illiam Wood
res. of Amer
an Woolen Co
our Employes
have been led
o believe the
reduction from
of hours from
56 to 54 was
an act of the
manufactures
where as the
IL PANE
PER
I
RAGAZZI

On the morning of January 12, city officials sounded a riot call on the bells of city hall in Lawrence for the first time in the city's history.

The call required the presence of every police officer in the city; regular, special and reserve. . . . *The mill workers were marching from the mills!*

Starting in the huge Everett mill, thousands had stopped work when they saw their pay-checks. The companies had uniformly taken advantage of the new Massachusetts law which went into effect January 1. They had cut the work hours, yes.

But they also had cut wages to match while, at the same time, speeding up production!

100

AVERAGE ANNUAL EARNINGS IN CERTAIN MASSACHUSETTS CITIES AND TOWNS FOR THREE SELECTED INDUSTRIES [1]

Cities and Towns	Population (1900)	Boots and Shoes		Cotton Goods		Foundry and Machine Shop	
		Number of Employees	Average Annual Earnings	Number of Employees	Average Annual Earnings	Number of Employees	Average Annual Earnings
Boston.......	560,892	....	....	....	....	3,229	$681.47
Worcester....	118,421	764	$543.32	227	$433.74	4,250	598.06
Fall River....	104,863	....	....	24,225	447.40	547	507.45
Lowell......	94,969	1,064	453.40	10,955	444.77	1,935	497.67
Lynn........	68,513	13,038	596.47			266	640.98
Lawrence.....	62,559	....	....	4,422	437.54	867	578.49
Brockton.....	40,063				....	146	690.03
Chelsea......	34,072				....	....	....
Beverly......	13,884				....	....	....
Peabody.....	11,523				....	345	639.95
Milford......	11,376				....	....	....
Weymouth ...	11,324				....	....	....
Garden.......	10,813				....	103	497.84
Natuck.......	9,488				....	....	....
Rockland.....	5,327				....	....	....

[1] Statistics of .... ston, 1909. Pp. 12–32.

Pay Envelopes

The Bost

VOL LXXXI–NO 29.   BOSTON. MONDAY

PANORAMIC PHOTOGRAPH OF LAWRENCE
BY STRIKE OF OPERATIVES, WHO.

Pacific   Atlantic   Lower Pacific   Washington   Pe

STRIKERS TO MAKE FIRM STAND TODAY

Plan to Do All They Can to Swell Their Ranks at Lawrence.

To Start With Huge Parade to Deter

CARDINAL DUE TO
AT NOON TO

Directions for Parade After Wireless From t

Daily Globe.

JARY 29, 1912—SIXTEEN PAGES. COPYRIGHT, 1912, BY THE GLOBE NEWSPAPER CO. **PRICE TWO CENTS.**

ERE INDUSTRY IS PARALYZED
IS TO BE PUT TO THE SUPREME TEST TODAY.

ood   Ayer   Electric Light Station   Farrell's Bleachery   Lawrence Dye Works   Prospect   Paper Mills

LPS FUND IS INCREASED

dayContributions well the Total.

Grateful for Aid in Behalf of Children.

ly Home Occupied Without Leave.

PITTSFIELD LOSS $235,000 FIRE TO BE INVESTIGATED

Five Persons Hurt---Business Section Menaced For Hours---Area Without Heat Today.

Workers by the thousands left the Wood mill, the Ayer mill, the Arlington mill. Soon 25,000 workers from eleven mills had started their strike. The power was shut down. *Not a wheel turned!*

The great mills—largest in the world—had *stopped production*. . . .

Even the children joined the strike.

Leaderless, the men, women and children milled through the streets. It was mid-winter with below-freezing temperature. When the workers sought to set up a picket line in front of a plant, the company sprayed them with freezing cold water.

When angry women strikers met a policeman on a bridge, they stripped him of his uniform and were about to throw him into the canal, when he escaped.

The local police were incited to use force on the strikers. Meeting with Mayor Michael Scanlon, the strikers were told to "go back to work." The mill owners, led by William M. Wood, refused even to listen to the strikers' grievances.

"There is no strike in Lawrence. Just mob rule," stated Mr. Wood.

Two days later, Joseph J. Ettor arrived in the city upon the invitation of the strikers. Ettor, a young Italian-American from New York, was a leader of the then growing Industrial Workers of the World, a militant movement of working people believing in "one big union."

Addressing the strikers upon his arrival, he told them:
"The labor problem cannot be quenched by a fire hose. . . . Our strength rests on our unity."

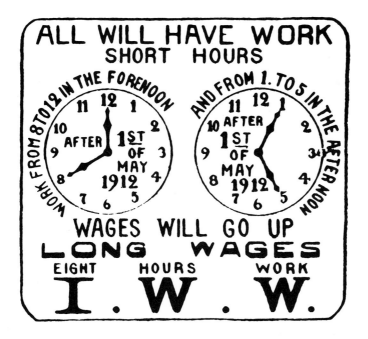

When the strikers appealed for a settlement, the answer was the calling of the state militia into Lawrence. It was the first time in Massachusetts history that the militia was used in a labor dispute. More than 50 militia companies saw service before the 63-day strike ended.

"The managers of the mills," said the *American Wool and Cotton Reporter*, a big business magazine, *"have rendered great service by their refusal to yield to threats of disorder and destruction by anarchistic leaders like Joseph J. Ettor."*

"But they cannot weave cloth with bayonets," Ettor told the people. *By all means make this strike as peaceful as possible. In the last analysis, all the blood spilled will be your blood."*

114

Uniting all workers was the big aim. *"Solidarity is necessary,"* Ettor told the strikers. *"Division is the surest means to lose the strike. . . . Among workers there is only one nationality, one race, one creed. . . . Remember always that you are workers with interests against those of the mill owners. . . . There are but two races, the race of useful members of society and the race of useless ones."*

118

Arturo Giovannitti

The IWW sent its best organizers to Lawrence. Arturo Giovannitti, well-known Italian-American editor and author, arrived on the scene from New York. So did Elizabeth Gurley Flynn, IWW organizer, who had just come from the west coast.

Elizabeth Gurley Flynn, Bill Haywood and Joseph Ettor

Bill Haywood also came to Lawrence, direct from union campaigns in the Northwest.

A militant leader of mine workers, Haywood's arrival caused what was described by the *Lawrence Tribune* as *"The greatest demonstration ever accorded a visitor in Lawrence."* More than 15,000 people greeted him.

THE GREATEST DEMONSTRATION EVER ACCORDED A "VISITOR" IN LAWRENCE—*Lawrence Tribune.*

The immediate job for the strikers was to get the strike organized. A strike committee of 12 members was elected including Joe Ettor. This committee was responsible to a general strike committee of 56 members. This committee in turn was responsible to 27 different groups of strikers, established on the basis of nationality, since language was an important factor in the strike organization.

"And behind each committee was a substitute committee," stated Haywood. Demands were formulated by democratic vote. . . .
—A 15 per cent wage increase.
—Time and one-half overtime for work over 56 hours a week.
—No premium system.
—No discrimination in rehiring after the strike.
Mass picketing of some 6,000 workers at the factory gates and meetings on the town common (at which all speeches were translated into a dozen different languages) took place daily.

HOLLIDAY   BORN   SMITH   ADAMSON
(Weaver)   (Finisher)   (Percher)   (Dresser)

GANINITTI   BIANKOSKY   BEDARD   WELZENBACH   ED RILEY, Chairman
(Comber)   (Comber)   (Fin. Secty.)   (Mender)   (Percher)

THE COMMITTEE OF TEN WHICH MET THE MILL BOSSES—AND WON.   JOE ETTOR WAS THE
TENTH MEMBER.

"The strikers handled their own affairs," states Haywood. *"It was a democracy. . . . All the workers in connection with the strike were picked from material that in the mill was regarded as worth no more than $6 to $7 a week. . . ."*

Six stores were set up by the strikers, 11 soup kitchens, 120 relief investigators, a fund-raising committee. . . .

Each family was allowed $2 to $5.50 a week for food and $1.50 every two weeks for fuel and clothing.

Two doctors voluntarily gave medical aid throughout the strike.

128

It was a new kind of strike. A singing strike. Song overcame all language barriers. Included among the nationalities involved in the strike were Americans from Poland, Portugal, Lithuania, Syria, Armenia, France, Greece, Turkey, Russia, Italy, Ireland, Canada, Germany.

There was even a song—especially written by the IWW poet Joe Hill—critical of AFL Textile President John Golden. . . .

130

CASEY JONES—THE UNION SCAB

I.W.W. SONGS

HOLD THE FORT

SOLIDARITY FOREVER!

JOHN GOLDEN AND THE LAWRENCE STRIKE

BY JOE HILL

*In Lawrence when the starving masses struck for more to eat
And wooden-headed Wood he tried the strikers to defeat,
To Sammy Gompers wrote and asked him what he thought,
And this is just the answer that the mailman brought.*

CHORUS

*A little talk with Golden
Makes it right, all right;
He'll settle any strike,
If there's coin in sight;
Just take him up to dine
And everything is fine—
A little talk with Golden
Makes it right, all right.*

Uniting the strikers meant winning the full support of the skilled workers, too.

Addressing a meeting of these workers, Ettor said: *"You are the skilled of the mills. You are paid more than the others to create a jealousy between the skilled and the unskilled, between the high-paid workers and the low-paid workers. You must either reach down and lift them up or they will reach up and pull you down."*

Instrumental in winning the support of the skilled workers for the strike was Mrs. Annie Welzenbach, young woman member known throughout the city as the most highly paid worker in the mills, earning $20 a week. Her slogan every day was *"Get out on the picket line."*

132

Mrs. Annie Welzenbach, one of the committee of ten and the highest paid worker in Lawrence mills.

The strikers and their leaders had to answer attacks on them as "advocates of violence," as "saboteurs" and "conspirators."

The mill owners' magazine, *American Wool and Cotton Reporter*, warned of "anarchy" and "socialism." "*Must we permit laborers to listen to a subtle anarchistic philosophy which challenges the fundamental idea of law and order?*" it was asked.

But Ettor told the workers: *"You can hope for no success on any policy of violence. . . . Violence necessarily means the loss of the strike."*

And even such prominent magazines as *Collier's* pointed out: *"It is wrong to charge . . . that the doctrine of the IWW—as it was preached at Lawrence—was fundamentally a doctrine of violence; fundamentally it was a doctrine of the brotherhood of man."*

However, the companies had other ideas on the question. *"I will allow no mass meetings,"* stated Col. E. LeRoy Sweetser, head of the militia. *"I will allow no parades. We are going to look for trouble. . . . We are not looking for peace now. . . ."*

Said Mayor Scanlon: *"We will either break this strike or break the strikers' heads."*

Said the companies: *"Go back to work and we will discuss your grievances later."*

Said a stockholder: *"The way to settle this strike is to shoot down 40 or 50 of 'em,"* reported Richard Washburn Child in *Collier's* of March, 1912.

136

On January 15 thirty-six strikers were arrested and jailed for one year . . . for throwing snowballs. As the city judge stated: *"The only way we can teach them is to deal out the severest sentences."*

But other lessons were also learned; *"The grievance of one is the grievance of all,"* the strikers said. And the picket lines—starting at 5:30 each morning—grew stronger.

"The very courts . . . supposed to be impartial," stated the strikers, *"are being used by the millionaire mill owners."*

Nor did the State Board of Arbitration, which entered the situation, help. The mill owners simply refused to meet.

138

Mr. Wood wrote the following letter to the strikers:

"To the Strikers:

"I am an employee of the Company as you are. . . .

"I ask you to return to work. . . .

"You are being advised by strangers . . . men who are not and never have been employees of the Company. . . .

"When conditions of our business warrant raising your wages, I shall, without even a request, recommend such an advance."

"Wm. W. Wood, President
American Woolen Co.
January 19, 1912"

And the strikers replied:

"To Mr. Wood:
   "We are of the opinion that you have had ample time to consider the demands of the men, women and children who have made the American Woolen Co. what it is today.
   "You speak of men from out of town who know nothing of the textile industry. . . . We, the committee, would like to know if the militia, the special policemen and the Pinkerton detectives, recently brought into the city, know anything about the textile industry."

"Strike Committee"

Rep. Calvin Coolidge of Northampton

Governor Eugene N. Foss of Massachusetts, himself a mill owner who had ordered 12 companies of state militia to the strike scene, made a proposal to the strikers:

—*"Go back . . . in the mills . . . for 30 days and negotiate a settlement. . . . Not the slightest approach to anarchy will be tolerated."*

The strikers rejected the offer. So did the mill owners, stating: *"To comply with the request of the governor . . . would be to offer a premium . . . for anarchy and murder."*

Governor Foss then named a committee from the State Legislature to investigate the strike. It was headed by the young Calvin Coolidge of Northampton, later to become President of the United States. But the committee accomplished very little.

Governor Eugene N. Foss of Massachusetts

On January 20 dynamite was discovered by the police in three separate locations in Lawrence. Said the *New York Times*, as the newspapers throughout the nation screamed anti-labor headlines: *"When the strikers use or prepare to use dynamite, they display a fiendish lack of humanity."*

Urban Di Prato, the shoemaker, in whose shop a bundle of dynamite was found.

But a few days later the newspapers were compelled to admit the whole "dynamite threat" was a hoax. It was, as Samuel Gompers reported to the AFL membership, *"a conspiracy to discredit the textile strikers."*

It is *"easy to entertain the suspicion that the manufacturers tried to get strikers falsely condemned for using explosives,"* stated the *Philadelphia Record*.

"To attempt to make it appear that the Lawrence strikers were preparing to blow up the mills and kill innocent people by dynamite explosions," stated the *New York Evening Post, "is an offense on the part of capitalism which pales the worst acts ever committed by labor unions."*

Said the *Iron Age: "It was a dastardly piece of work and those concerned in it . . . have betrayed the cause of employers generally, by supplying a basis on which hereafter allegations by strikers against unscrupulous and lawless acts of employers will be received with credence. . . . "*

Eight strikers were arrested, charged with the crime. The finding of dynamite was immediately used as reason for closing the streets to picketing in front of the mills.

146

As the *Schenectady Gazette* reported on January 30: *"John J. Breen, a member of the school board, son of former Mayor John Breen and one of the most prominent citizens of Lawrence, was arrested by the state police tonight charged with 'conspiracy to mar, deface and destroy property.' The police alleged that he 'planted' dynamite. . . . "*

Breen was subsequently tried and found guilty. He was fined $500. It was not until later that even more sensational facts were to be revealed.

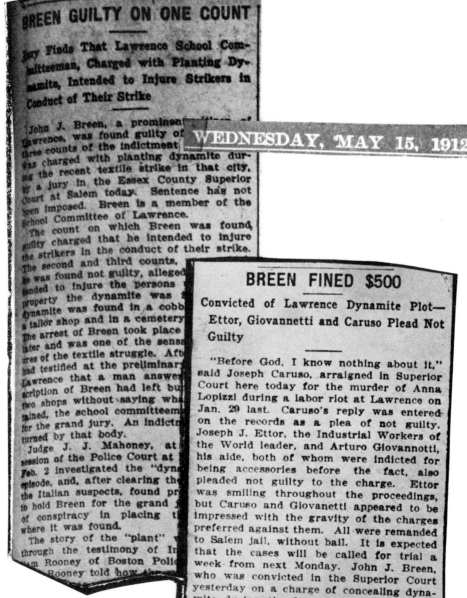

BREEN GUILTY ON ONE COUNT

Jury Finds That Lawrence School Committeeman, Charged with Planting Dynamite, Intended to Injure Strikers in Conduct of Their Strike

John J. Breen, a prominent citizen of Lawrence, was found guilty of three counts of the indictment was charged with planting dynamite during the recent textile strike in that city, by a jury in the Essex County Superior Court at Salem today. Sentence has not been imposed. Breen is a member of the School Committee of Lawrence.

The count on which Breen was found guilty charged that he intended to injure the strikers in the conduct of their strike. The second and third counts, he was found not guilty, alleged tended to injure the persons property the dynamite was dynamite was found in a cobb a tailor shop and in a cemetery The arrest of Breen took place later and was one of the sensa ures of the textile struggle. Aft had testified at the preliminary Lawrence that a man answer scription of Breen had left bu two shops without saying wha tained, the school committeem for the grand jury. An indictm turned by that body.

Judge J. J. Mahoney, at session of the Police Court at Feb. 2 investigated the "dyn episode, and, after clearing th the Italian suspects, found pr to hold Breen for the grand j of conspiracy in placing t where it was found.

The story of the "plant" through the testimony of In am Rooney of Boston Poli Rooney told how

WEDNESDAY, MAY 15, 1912

BREEN FINED $500

Convicted of Lawrence Dynamite Plot— Ettor, Giovannetti and Caruso Plead Not Guilty

"Before God, I know nothing about it," said Joseph Caruso, arraigned in Superior Court here today for the murder of Anna Lopizzi during a labor riot at Lawrence on Jan. 29 last. Caruso's reply was entered on the records as a plea of not guilty. Joseph J. Ettor, the Industrial Workers of the World leader, and Arturo Giovannotti, his aide, both of whom were indicted for being accessories before the fact, also pleaded not guilty to the charge. Ettor was smiling throughout the proceedings, but Caruso and Giovanetti appeared to be impressed with the gravity of the charges preferred against them. All were remanded to Salem jail, without bail. It is expected that the cases will be called for trial a week from next Monday. John J. Breen, who was convicted in the Superior Court yesterday on a charge of concealing dynamite during the Lawrence labor troubles, was fined $500 by Judge Brown today.

and Giovannitti were transferred Essex County Jail in Lawrence to x County House of Correction at Salem today. The trip from Lawrence to Salem was accomplished quietly and few persons knew that it was being Giovanni

THURSDAY, MAY 16, 1912

In rapid succession, the mill owners tried a series of new efforts to break the strike. A group of men, disguised as workers but—according to the strikers—hired from the Burns and Pinkerton detective agencies, were imported from Boston. These agents sought to start a riot, broke windows in street cars.

But the strikers retained their discipline. *"The street cars were smashed by the thugs and agents of the mill owners,"* Ettor declared.

Shortly after that, the American Woolen Co. proposed separate settlements. The offer was rejected. *"The power of the capitalists is based on property,"* said Ettor. *"They have the laws, the army, everything! In spite of all that, the workers have something still more powerful. The workers' power . . . is the common bond of solidarity. . . . "*

Following the trolley-car provocation, the rumor was circulated that the strike was over. A "back to work" movement began.

It was necessary to mobilize a special demonstration of strikers to spread the word "No work Monday." The demonstration was a huge success. The plants remained shut tight. . . .

"This strike would be settled in 15 minutes if it wasn't for the haughty attitude of William M. Wood," stated Ettor.

154

Parade of strikers. The children shown here are not school kids on a holiday but actual mill workers.

At this stage a "Citizens committee" was formed of local citizens including mill owners who spread the idea that *"Ettor is a believer in the philosophy of force."* The strikers were urged to abandon a "hopeless" strike.

"Ettor is teaching sedition and treason to the institutions of the Commonwealth of Massachusetts," the committee stated.

But U.S. Senator Miles Poindexter from Washington differed, saying: *"The trouble has been caused by the presence of the militia."*

Meanwhile, the mill owners kept their machines running—although no cloth was being woven—in an attempt to deceive the strikers. A *New York Times* eyewitness reported, *"In the spinning room, every belt was in motion . . . yet not a single operative was at work. . . ."*

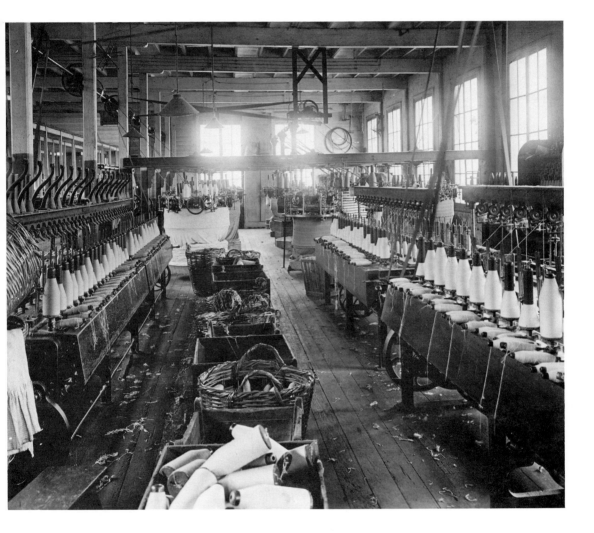

The newspapers were usually a source of confusion to the strikers and of comfort to the mill owners.

Strikers were usually referred to as an "unruly mob."

A Boston newspaper announced the finding of dynamite before the police had even started their search.

A newspaperman cried "fire" when armed militia, guns cocked, were facing a mass of peaceful picketing strikers.

Every leader of the strikers was termed an "anarchist" and an "agitator" and a "fomentor of violence."

As Samuel Gompers wrote for the AFL membership: *"Boston reporters did their best to try to manufacture daily stories about outbreaks between soldiers·and strikers. . . ."*

With production at a standstill, the mill owners were unable to break the unity of their striking employees. But a new incident occurred that was to deprive the strikers of their leaders. . . .

On the evening of January 29 police and troopers clashed with a group of strikers at Union and Garden Streets.

Ordered to disperse, the strikers found themselves faced with troopers on one side and police on the other. At that moment a shot rang out in the winter night. A young woman striker—Annie LoPizza—fell dead.

The strikers maintained that a police officer fired the shot.

Said Ettor, who had been speaking in another part of town when the tragedy happened, *"My sister, Annie LoPizza, was murdered by the agents of the mill owners."*

Next day Joseph Ettor and his companion, Arturo Giovannitti, were arrested, charged—though they insisted they were elsewhere when the murder took place—with being "access-ories."

"Both men were two miles away during the conflict," stated the author Mary Heaton Vorse in *Harpers Weekly*.

From that day on a new point was added to the strikers' list of demands: *"Free Ettor and Giovannitti!"*

Bill Haywood, who had left Lawrence to help raise funds, now returned and assumed the leadership of the strike. *"They cannot break our ranks,"* he told the strikers, *"as long as we retain our unity."*

168

'The worst thief is he whc steals the playtime of children.'
W.D.HAYWOOD.

JOIN THE I W. W. AND HELP PUT THE THIEVES TO WORK

Haywood, a big man who had lost his right eye in an accident when a child, held meetings regularly with the strikers, especially meetings of women and of children.

At a children's strike meeting Haywood remarked bitterly: *"These kids should be in school instead of slaving in the mills. . . .*
These children have been starving from birth. They have been starved in their mothers' wombs. And their mothers have been starving before the children were conceived."

So frequent had been the police attacks on the picket-line, that the women conceived of an idea. Meeting with Haywood, a group of women strikers suggested that the pregnant women strikers head the picket-line.

"You let the women go first," one woman said. "They won't attack us women with big bellies."

With tears in his eyes and against his better judgement, Haywood agreed. Next morning the police attacked the line. "They would not allow the women to escape," reported an eye-witness. Two women had miscarriages.

From then on the men took over the picket line. . . .

172

When workers sought to attend the funeral of Annie LoPizza a few days later, troopers from Troop H, Squad 1, of Boston rode their horses into the mourners. There could be no funeral.

Nearby Harvard University allowed students credits for their midterm examinations if they agreed to serve in the militia against the strikers. *"Insolent, well-fed Harvard men,"* the *New York Call* reported, *"parade up and down, their rifles loaded . . . their bayonets glittering. . . . "*

On January 30 another tragedy occurred. A 16-year-old boy, a non-striker, was bayoneted by a trooper and died. John Rami, according to testimony later, had refused to "move on" when a trooper told him to.

Even many members of the militia were revolted by the attacks on the people. *"I didn't go into the militia for this,"* said one soldier in a magazine interview. *"I had always supposed that militia were used in strikes to quell riots and not to patrol the mill district and keep strikers away from it."*

174

Meanwhile, preliminary hearings in the trial of Joe Ettor and Arturo Giovannitti were started.

Attempts were made by the prosecution to influence the trial by smearing the IWW, accusing it of "fomenting violence."

Early in the case William Haywood was called to testify by the prosecution. Haywood, as well as other IWW leaders, refused to answer questions, availing himself of provisions of the Fifth Amendment of the Constitution:

"It is well known," stated Haywood to the court, in regard to a question put him by the prosecution, *"but I propose to remain silent on all questions that might incriminate myself or prejudice the public or the jury against these defendants."*

176

HAYWOOD WILL NOT JEOPARDIZE HIMSELF

Called as State Witness at Lawrence, Refuses to Speak Against Ettor.

JOSEPH ETTOR.
Leader of Strikers at Lawrence.

WILLIAM D. HAYWOOD,
Witness at Lawrence Hearing.

Support for the Lawrence strike came from all over the nation. About $1,000 a day was received to aid the strikers and their families. From cities and towns from coast to coast the donations and expressions of support mounted daily. Especially from industrial communities—from Lynn, Mass., Schenectady, N. Y., Erie, Pa., Detroit, Chicago and from the far northwest— working people expressed their solidarity.

As support mounted, the Executive Council of the American Federation of Labor unanimously approved a resolution of solidarity. And, while Gov. Foss sent militia from such towns as nearby Salem, Lynn and Lowell, the working people of these communities sent food, clothes, funds and even—from Lowell farmers—a live cow.

A PROCLAMATION !

IS MASSACHUSETTS IN AMERICA ?

Ready to plunge the bayonets into woman's blood

Military Law Declared in Massachusetts !

Habeas Corpus Denied in Massachusetts !

Free Speech Throttled in Massachusetts !

Free Assemblage Outlawed in Massachusetts !

Unlawful Seizure of Persons in Massachusetts !

Unwarranted Search of Homes in Massachusetts !

Right to Bear Arms Questioned in Massachusetts !

Mill Owners Resort to Dynamite Plots and Violence in Massachusetts !

Militia Hired to Break Strike in Massachusetts !

Innocent People Killed by Militia in Massachusetts !

Militia Ordered to Shoot to Kill in Mass. !

Unusual Bail and Fines Exacted in Massachusetts !

Corporations Control Administrations in Mass. !

The striking textile workers of Lawrence, Massachusetts are confronted with the above described conditions. They are making a noble fight for an increase of wages and to prevent discriminations against the members of the organization carrying on the strike. To abolish a pernicious premium system inaugurated for no other purpose than the speeding up of already overworked workers. If you want to assist the strikers send funds to JOSEPH BEDARD, 9 Mason Street, Franco-Belgian Hall, Financial Secretary Textile Workers Industrial Union, Lawrence, Massachusetts.

To safeguard the health of small children during the strike, parents would send them to relatives and friends in other cities. Small tots were bundled up, with identification tags hung around their necks, and sent off to spend a few weeks in New York or Bridgeport or Barre, Vt., or Philadelphia. Usually a reception demonstration would be given the children upon their arrival in a community.

Arrival of children at Grand Central Station, N.Y.

The children would be fed and clothed while away. Every one of the 119 kids sent to "strike parents" in New York in February *"was found to be suffering from malnutrition in some form."*

Children at the Labor Temple, New York City

The children were, of course, greatly missed while they were away. . . .

Lawrence le 28 Février 1912

Chère Adrienne et chère Marie
Je vous écris ses quelques lignes
pour vous dire que nous avons
reçus votre Portrait nous som-
me heureuse de voir que vous
êtes si bien posser ainsi que
vous avez une si toil . le
et des si bel
n'avez jama
été maintein
pas sus dor
nuit de joi
tément en
êter si bell
maintenant
que ta g'èr

Lawrence February 28 1912
Dear Adrienne and Dear Marie
    I write to you these few
lines to tell you that we
have received your picture
and that we feel very happy
to see that you look so well
and that you have such beautiful dresses and such nice
shoes. You never were as
beautiful as you are now.
    We could not sleep all
night for joy and happiness
to know that you are so
nice. We hope the stroke
will be soon . . . .

But it was found that the sending away of the children was giving heart to the strikers. There were fewer mouths to feed.

Stated Col. E. LeRoy Sweetser, commanding troops in Lawrence: *"I will not permit the shipping off of little children."*

On the morning of February 24, when the strike was in its 43rd day, another group of strikers' children gathered at the Lawrence railroad station to leave for Philadelphia. There were some 40 children in all gathered there, saying tearful farewells to their parents when . . .

. . . without warning, the parents and children were ferociously attacked, beaten and thrown by the police into waiting patrol wagons.

Observers were to testify later before a Congressional committee:

"I saw them take little children and pick them up by the leg and throw them in the patrol wagon. . . ."

"I saw one military policeman with a club strike a woman, a pregnant woman, over the abdomen."

BAR SHIPMENT OF STRIKE CHILDREN; WOMEN CLUBBED

Youngsters Trampled in Riot When Lawrence Police Halt Exportation.

MOTHERS FIGHT WITH TEETH AND HATPINS

Authorities Descend on Station Where One Hundred Little Ones Were to Entrain for Philadelphia.

THE NEW YORK HERALD.

Women and children—bleeding and injured—were taken to the jail and locked up.

Said the Boston *"Common"* of February 28: *"Police, acting under orders of the city marshal, clubbed, choked and knocked down women and children, the innocent wives and babies of the strikers."*

The nation stood aghast. . . .

190

CLINTON, IND., *February 27, 1912.*

Hon. VICTOR L. BERGER:

Whereas the police and militia system of the city of Lawrence and the State of Massachusetts, instigated by the highly protected interests of that city, did, in a brutal and un-American way, club men and women, regardless of sex or condition, forcibly reminding one of the Cossacks of Russia, for exercising their rights as American citizens.

Therefore we demand that this inhuman and barbarous practice be immediately discontinued, and that the Congress and President of the United States take such steps as are necessary to bring these violators of law to an accounting.

THOMAS J. LLEWELLYN,
THOMAS PRICE,
ROB BROWN,
WILLIAM H. REED,
Subdistrict of the United Mine Workers.
[Telegram.]

NEW YORK, *March 1, 1912.*

Hon. VICTOR BERGER,
House of Representatives, Washington, D. C.:

Not since the days of negro slavery has there occurred so flagrant an outrage on personal liberty as that exhibited in the treatment of the Lawrence strikers by the local and State authorities in forbidding parents from sending their children to friends and sympathizers. The attack of the police upon the mothers of the children was an act of brutality which aroused the indignation of every public-spirited citizen. The situation is aggravating by the fact that these women were from a foreign country and had come to America expecting to find the high standard of living and regard for personal liberty of which we boast, on which our Republic is founded. They have found neither. In the name of the 55,000 working people of New York, the Women's Trade Union League of that city urges upon Congress the passage of the bill calling for immediate action of Congress and the Federal authorities.

MARY E. DREIER, *President.*

CENTRAL TRADES AND LABOR UNION OF ST. LOUIS AND VICINITY,
St. Louis, Mo., February 28, 1912.

Hon. VICTOR L. BERGER,
Member House of Representatives, Washington, D. C.

DEAR SIR: In compliance with instructions received from the Central Trades and Labor Union of St. Louis, Mo., the undersigned respectfully submits the following for your careful consideration:

To the House of Representatives, Washington, D. C.

GENTLEMEN: The St. Louis Central Trades and Labor Union of St. Louis, representing 50,000 men and women, respectfully asks Congress to forthwith investigate the horrible state of affairs in Lawrence, Mass., and take such steps as will without delay call a halt to the corporation anarchy of the mill owners under the protection of the municipal administration and the State militia.

Respectfully,

[SEAL.]

DAVID KREYLING, *Secretary.*

The strikers responded to the attack. The picket line was at its largest. The unity of the workers was unbreakable.

Outstanding Americans spoke out against the mill owners and for the strikers. . . .

Boardman Robinson, termed by the *New York Times "one of America's most penetrating cartoonists,"* reacted in a bitter drawing in the old *New York Tribune.*

Esteemed citizens from all walks of life backed the strikers. Professor Vida D. Scudder of Wellesley College wrote: *"I would rather never again wear a thread of woolen than know my garments had been woven at the cost of such misery as I have seen."*

Congressman William B. Wilson of Pennsylvania, a founder of the United Mine Workers, and later the first Secretary of Labor, condemned the mill owners and led an investigation.

"It is an outrage," stated the celebrated writer William Dean Howells. *"Could anyone think it was anything else?"*

Senator William Borah termed it an *"invasion of Constitutional privileges"* and called for an investigation.

Frederick W. Lehmann, chairman of the American Bar Association and legal adviser to President Taft, stated: *"The act was in violation of . . . Constitutional rights."*

194

AT LAWRENCE

Boardman Robinson

These children must remain at home in want because it would be a case of "neglect" to send them away to strike sympathizers.
—New York Tribune, Feb. 28, 1912

William Allen White, famed journalist: *"There was no excuse for the violence by police."*

Mayor Newton D. Baker of Cleveland: *"Americans will not countenance such war against labor."*

Judge Ben Lindsey of Denver: *"Big business has thrown off its mask in the Lawrence strike."*

Mayor George R. Lunn of Schenectady, N.Y.: *"Every right supposedly guaranteed under the Constitution has been ruthlessly taken from the industrial slaves of Lawrence."*

U.S. Senator Miles Poindexter: *"I never expected to see such things in the U.S.A."*

"I want to call attention," stated Rep. Victor Berger, first Socialist Congressman ever elected to Congress, *"to one of the most outrageous invasions of Constitutional rights that has ever occurred in this country. I refer to the brutal manhandling and clubbing of women and children in Lawrence, Massachusetts, by the official and unofficial agents of the Wool trust."*

"It is not always a disgrace to be arrested. Sometimes it is an honor to be arrested."
—*Congressman Victor Berger*

As a result of popular indignation and a demand for a Congressional investigation, the U.S. Congress called for the facts.

A delegation of 16 child strikers from Lawrence appeared before the committee in Washington.

62D CONGRESS }
2d Session }

HOUSE OF REPRESENTATIVES

{ DOCUMENT
{ No. 671

THE STRIKE AT LAWRENCE, MASS.

HEARINGS

BEFORE

THE COMMITTEE ON RULES

OF THE

HOUSE OF REPRESENTATIVES

ON

HOUSE RESOLUTIONS 409 AND 433

MARCH 2-7, 1912

WASHINGTON
GOVERNMENT PRINTING OFFICE
1912

So great was the national indignation that the first lady of the land, Mrs. Helen Taft, attended the Washington hearings and heard for herself the facts about the Lawrence struggle. . . .

"They make us go quicker and quicker all the time," a 14-year-old boy told the Committee.

"As soon as I came home, I had to go to sleep, I was so tired," the Congressmen were told by a 15-year-old girl.

Master MURPHY. If you are late two minutes, they close the door, or for seven minutes. They take off an hour's pay.

The CHAIRMAN. Were you at the station Saturday morning, the 24th day of February?

Master MURPHY. No, sir.

The CHAIRMAN. Any other questions? You can stand aside.

STATEMENT OF PETER STUDIES.

The CHAIRMAN. How old are you, Peter?

Master STUDIES. Fourteen and four months.

The CHAIRMAN. How many are there in your family?

Master STUDIES. One small girl.

The CHAIRMAN. One small girl and yourself?

Master STUDIES. And me makes two.

The CHAIRMAN. And you make two?

Master STUDIES. Yes, sir.

The CHAIRMAN. Where do you work?

Master STUDIES. American Woolen Co.

The CHAIRMAN. How long have you worked there?

Master STUDIES. Four months.

The CHAIRMAN. Talk louder. What do you do? What sort of work?

Master STUDIES. Bobbin boy.

The CHAIRMAN. How much pay do you get per week?

Master STUDIES. $5.10.

The CHAIRMAN. What is the smallest pay you would get for four days' work?

Master STUDIES. $4.

The CHAIRMAN. $4? $4 or $3?

Master STUDIES. $3, sometimes I get.

The CHAIRMAN. That is the smallest you get?

Master STUDIES. Yes, sir.

The CHAIRMAN. Do you have to pay anything for water?

Master STUDIES. 10 cents a week.

The CHAIRMAN. 10 cents a week. Do they ever work you overtime without pay?

Master STUDIES. Saturdays we have to sweep the room, and you work about an hour, and they don't pay you.

The CHAIRMAN. I can't hear you.

Master STUDIES. Saturdays you have to sweep the room up, and they don't pay you at all.

The CHAIRMAN. Is your father living?

Master STUDIES. No; he is dead.

The CHAIRMAN. Is your mother alive?

Master STUDIES. Yes, sir.

The CHAIRMAN. Does anybody else in the family do any work except you?

Master STUDIES. My mother and two boarders.

The CHAIRMAN. Your mother and two boar—

STATEMENT OF CAMELLA TEOLI.

The CHAIRMAN. Camella, how old are you?

Miss TEOLI. Fourteen years and eight months.

The CHAIRMAN. Fourteen years and eight months?

Miss TEOLI. Yes.

The CHAIRMAN. How many children are there in your family?

Miss TEOLI. Five.

The CHAIRMAN. Where do you work?

Miss TEOLI. In the woolen mill.

The CHAIRMAN. For the American Woolen Co.?

Miss TEOLI. Yes.

The CHAIRMAN. What sort of work do you do?

Miss TEOLI. Twisting.

The CHAIRMAN. You do twisting?

Miss TEOLI. Yes.

The CHAIRMAN. How much do you get a week?

Miss TEOLI. $6.55.

The CHAIRMAN. What is the smallest pay?

Miss TEOLI. $2.64.

The CHAIRMAN. Do you have to pay anything for water?

Miss TEOLI. Yes.

The CHAIRMAN. How much?

Miss TEOLI. 10 cents every two weeks.

The CHAIRMAN. Do they hold back any of your pay?

Miss TEOLI. No.

The CHAIRMAN. Have they ever held back any?

Miss TEOLI. One week's pay.

The CHAIRMAN. They have held back one week's pay?

Miss TEOLI. Yes.

The CHAIRMAN. Does your father work, and where?

Miss TEOLI. My father works in the Washington.

The CHAIRMAN. The Washington Woolen Mill?

Miss TEOLI. Yes, sir.

The CHAIRMAN. How much pay does he get for a week's work?

Miss TEOLI. $7.70.

The CHAIRMAN. Does he always work a full week?

Miss TEOLI. No.

The CHAIRMAN. Well, how often does it happen that he does not work a full week?

Miss TEOLI. He works in the winter a full week, and usually he don't in the summer.

The CHAIRMAN. In the winter he works a full week, and in the summer how much?

Miss TEOLI. Two or three days a week.

The CHAIRMAN. What sort of work does he do?

Miss TEOLI. He is a comber.

The CHAIRMAN. Now, did you ever get hurt in the mill?

Miss TEOLI. Yes.

The CHAIRMAN. Can you tell the committee about that—how it happened and what it was?

Miss TEOLI. Yes.

The CHAIRMAN. Tell us about it now, in your own way.

Miss Teoli. Well, I used to go to school, and then a man came up to my house and asked my father why I didn't go to work, so my father says I don't know whether she is 13 or 14 years old. So, the man say you give me $4 and I will make the papers come from the old country saying you are 14. So, my father gave him the $4, and in one month came the papers that I was 14. I went to work, and about two weeks got hurt in my head.

The Chairman. Now, how did you get hurt, and where were you hurt in the head; explain that to the committee?

Miss Teoli. I got hurt in Washington.

The Chairman. In the Washington Mill?

Miss Teoli. Yes, sir.

The Chairman. What part of your head?

Miss Teoli. My head.

The Chairman. Well, how were you hurt?

Miss Teoli. The machine pulled the scalp off.

The Chairman. The machine pulled your scalp off?

Miss Teoli. Yes, sir.

The Chairman. How long ago was that?

Miss Teoli. A year ago, or about a year ago.

The Chairman. Were you in the hospital after that?

Miss Teoli. I was in the hospital seven months.

The Chairman. Seven months?

Miss Teoli. Yes.

The Chairman. Did the company pay your bills while you were in the hospital?

Miss Teoli. Yes, sir.

The Chairman. The company took care of you?

Miss Teoli. The company only paid my bills; they didn't give me anything else.

The Chairman. They only paid your hospital bills; they did not give you any pay?

Miss Teoli. No, sir.

The Chairman. But paid the doctors' bills and hospital fees?

Miss Teoli. Yes, sir.

Mr. Lenroot. They did not pay your wages?

Miss Teoli. No, sir.

The Chairman. Did they arrest your father for having sent you to work for 14?

Miss Teoli. Yes, sir.

The Chairman. What did they do with him after they arrested him?

Miss Teoli. My father told this about the man he gave $4 to, and then they put him on again.

The Chairman. Are you still being treated by the doctors for the scalp wound?

Miss Teoli. Yes, sir.

The Chairman. How much longer do they tell you you will have to be treated?

Miss Teoli. They don't know.

The Chairman. They do not know?

Miss Teoli. No.

The Chairman. Are you working now?

Miss Teoli. Yes, sir.

Public pressure was aroused. President Taft ordered an investigation of industrial conditions in the nation.

The strike committee sounded an appeal for continued determination as victory loomed in sight. . . .

Although the strike had been on for almost two months, more than 10,000 men, women and children strikers were still on the picket line.

STAND FIRM! STAND FIRM! WIN EVERYTHING! WIN ALL! NOW IS THE TIME TO STICK!

The textile manufacturers are yielding!

The strike is nearly won; it will be won!

The brutality of the agents of the employers, police, militia, courts, and thugs has aroused the whole Nation!

The world is with us! We will, we must win!

All was silent when we suffered!

But now, now, the echo of the industrial struggle for more bread has aroused the citizens of the United States, and all the workers of the world!

The Senate of the United States has voiced the cries of protest of the maltreated textile workers! They are investigating!

Congress, aroused by the fiendish, savage treatment of pregnant women, of innocent babes, responds to the thunderous voice of an aroused Nation. They are investigating; they are acting, and the sores and wounds of our suffering and brutalized wives and children has laid bare the outrages of capitalist tyranny run mad and amuck!

President Taft, though little affected when we pleaded for redress against the wrongs, has heard the rumblings of a coming revolt, and he has acted only now as the servant of all the people!

Federal investigation by the Department of Justice, the Department of Commerce and Labor, the Department of Interstate Commerce, and by others, in response to our outcries against wrongs, shows that the Nation will no longer stand idly by and let cotton and woolen kings preserve a slavery worse than when the chattel slave was sold at the auction block!

We are winning; we have won!

Gov. Foss, frightened lest he may lose even the little respect that fair-minded people might have had for him, is backing down. The bloodhound of war, Col. Sweetser, is to be removed, and the reign by sword and bayonet in Lawrence is to cease!

We are winning; we have won!

A judge, servile tool of corporate interests, can no longer with immunity prostitute his office of trust to do the bidding for the tyrants and oppressors!

We are winning; we have won!

Forced by the unshaken solidarity of tens of thousands, backed by millions of workers, the manufacturers offer bribes, in small rations, to get their employees back to work; to end the reign of terror that they have inaugurated!

They are beaten; we are winning!

Everything is won except your claim for more pay and more rights as producers!

You will win that, too, but you must stand together as in the past!

Don't return to work until complete surrender by the oppressors and industrial czars is assured!

Don't break ranks, else the employers will break your necks and manhood later on!

All together! Let us win! Win all, win everything! Everybody on the fighting line! Everyone a fighter in this industrial war!

Nobody goes back to work until all go back together! Win! Win! Win!

From the Report on the Strike of Textile Workers in Lawrence, Mass., in 1912, U. S. Senate, 62 Congress, Document No. 870.

On March 12—sixty-three days after the workers had walked off their jobs—the mighty American Woolen Co., speaking for all Lawrence mills—surrendered.

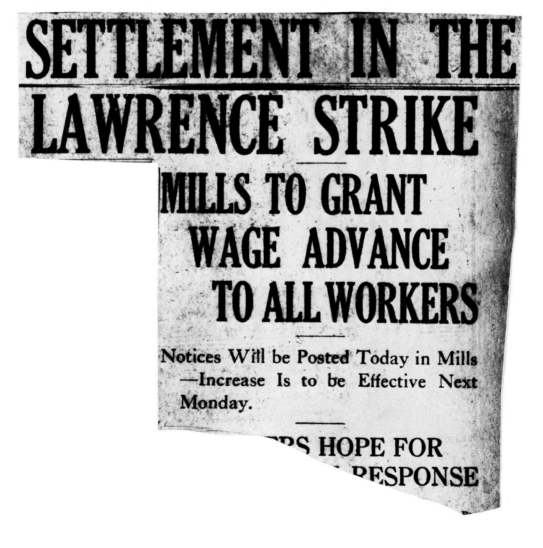

SETTLEMENT IN THE LAWRENCE STRIKE

MILLS TO GRANT WAGE ADVANCE TO ALL WORKERS

Notices Will be Posted Today in Mills —Increase Is to be Effective Next Monday.

ERS HOPE FOR
RESPONSE

The demands of the strikers were met in full. . . .

The strikers secured the following settlement from the American Woolen Co.
and much the same settlement from other mills:
—Time and one-quarter for overtime.
—All people on job work, 5 per cent increase flat.
—All those receiving less than 9½ cents per hour, an increase of 2 cents per
hour.
—All those receiving between 9½ and 10 cents an hour, an increase of 1¾ cents
per hour.
—All those receiving between 10 and 11 cents per hour, an increase of 1½ cents
per hour.
—All those receiving between 11 and 12 cents per hour, an increase of 1¼ cents
per hour.
—All those receiving between 12 and 20 cents per hour, an increase of 1 cent per
hour.
—No discrimination to be shown to anyone.
—Premiums to be given out every two weeks instead of every four, as
heretofore.

212

On March 14 some 25,000 men, women and children strikers gathered on Lawrence Common and solemnly voted on the settlement as they did on all other issues in the strike.

The strike was over. *And it had been won.*

"The women won the strike," said Haywood.

The 25,000 strikers won their raise, their improved conditions, and returned to work without discrimination, without the hated blacklist which mill owners used against strikers. . . .

214

"*The victory at Lawrence,*" stated Debs, who was to receive 900,000 votes that year for President of the United States on the Socialist ticket, "*one of the most decisive and far-reaching ever won by organized workers, demonstrated the power and invincibility of industrial unity backed by political solidarity.*"

"*Catholics, Jews, Protestants and unbelievers,*" wrote Mrs. Mary K. O'Sullivan, first woman organizer of the AFL, "*men and women of many races and languages, were working together as human beings with a common cause. . . . It was the most unselfish strike I have ever known. . . .*"

"*Labor has seldom, if ever, won so complete a victory,*" wrote the great journalist Lincoln Steffens, in the *New York Globe*.

"*The Lawrence strike is a clean cut triumph for the workers,*" stated the *Literary Digest* of March 23, 1912.

"*Few strikes involving so large a number of employees,*" said the U.S. Dept. of Labor, "*have continued with so little actual violence or riot.*"

216

Eugene Debs

"This strike since its inception has been in the hands of the strikers," Bill Haywood said. *"Every barbarity known to modern civilization has been perpetrated by police, military, courts and detectives. No one can point to any striker and say that he committed violence. They committed no violence except removing their hands . . .*

"But they removed those hands from the machinery," Haywood continued, *"and when they took those hands away from the wheels of the machinery, the machinery was dead."*

218

Soon after the strike was over the children returned.

Arriving on a special train, the children from New York, Barre, Vt., Philadelphia and elsewhere—little fugitives from the strike front—were met at the station by thousands of people. There were six brass bands.

Seven picnic wagons carred them from North Station to Ford's Hall, the former strike headquarters. More than 40,000 people joined in the welcome-home parade. Arriving, the children were embraced by their parents.

It was a welcome-home celebration not soon forgotten.

But also not to be forgotten were signs prominently displayed in the demonstration which carried the slogan: *"Open the jail gates or we will shut the mill gates."*

Because Ettor and Giovannitti were still in prison facing death in the electric chair. . . .

Elizabeth Gurley Flynn and Bill Haywood with returning children.

The Trial

It was months before, on January 30, that Joseph Ettor and Arturo Giovannitti, leaders of the strike, had been arrested and jailed without bail. The charge: "accessory" to the murder of a striker. Since that time the pair had been kept in prison, first in Lawrence and then in nearby Salem. A third victim was added when Joseph Caruso, a striker, was arrested, charged with the actual murder.

Both Ettor and Giovannitti insisted they were elsewhere when the shooting took place. Caruso, who was accused of having been influenced to commit the crime by Ettor and Giovannitti, stated he had never met or even heard either speak in his life.

On Sept. 27, 1912, as the three awaited trial a general protest strike was called, one of the great political mass strikes in U.S. history. Workers in Lawrence, Lynn, Mass., Barre, Vt., Haverhill, Mass., and other communities stopped work.

The demand was: *Free Ettor, Giovannitti and Caruso. Open the jail doors or we will close the mill gates.*

THE GENERAL STRIKE IS THE KEY THAT FITS THE LOCK TO FREEDOM

When the life or death trial of Ettor and Giovannitti opened at the Salem county courthouse on September 28, the entire building was alive with excitement over the general strike. The trial had to be postponed to find jurors who would serve. Ettor and Giovannitti were kept in open-topped cages throughout the trial . . . as if for fear the masses of people would rise and free them.

224

SCENE IN COURT AT LAWRENCE DURING
HEARING OF ETTOR AND GIOVANNITTI

Each day crowds of workers gathered outside the courthouse to cheer the prisoners as they were conducted to and from the trial room.

Both men, as well as Joseph Caruso, pleaded "not guilty."

And the entire world re-echoed their plea—and demanded justice in their case. More than $60,000 was collected by the Defense Committee. Protests arrived from Australia, Argentina, Canada, Hawaii, Sweden, Cuba, Panama, Italy. Giovannitti was nominated for the Italian parliament. Swedish workers urged an American boycott unless the men were freed. The French Confederation of Labor protested.

In America, the protest movement mounted. More than 5,000 workers attended a mass meeting in Pittsburgh. . . . Collections were taken up at meetings in Niles, Warren, Gerald and New Castle, Ohio. . . . The Granite Cutters of Barre, Vt., sent a donation. . . . Sharon, Pa., held a mass protest meeting. . . .

The newspaper of the Mexican-American labor movement in Los Angeles, *Regeneracion,* voiced support. . . . Lumberjacks in Harrison, La., sent a message. . . . So did 1,500 workers in Paterson, N. J. . . . More than 1,000 people in Lewiston, Maine, and 1,500 in Rumford, Maine, attended protest meetings and sent resolutions to Gov. Foss. . . . From San Francsico, Columbus, Cleveland, Detroit, Chicago, Minneapolis . . . the protests mounted. . . .

228

On Sept. 15 more than 17,000 people demonstrated on the Boston Common for freedom for Ettor and Giovannitti. After his address, Haywood was arrested on an old charge following the Lawrence strike.

Helen Keller, famed blind writer and liberal, wrote of Giovannitti: *"The crime with which he was charged was, of course, a legal fiction devised by the mill owners and their agents. Giovannitti's real crime was helping the strikers in their assault on the pocketbooks of the owners."*

Prof. William Taussig, respected Harvard economist, expressed his belief that *"Ettor was arrested to put him out of action."*

Dr. Harry Emerson Fosdick stated of Ettor: *"Although he was in no way concerned in the killing and although he himself was two miles away, he is held without bail and stands in danger of the electric chair."*

230

Helen Keller

About this time a bombshell landed on the Lawrence scene. William M. Wood, president of the American Woolen Co., was indicted in Boston, charged with being involved in the dynamite plot during the Lawrence strike. A friend of Wood's who built the famous Wood mill had committed suicide after confessing his connection with the crime.

The indictment of Wood rocked the nation. Newspapers, representing all opinions, considered it front page news, and it had a marked effect on the trial of Ettor and Giovannitti. When the trial finally was held later, Wood was acquitted. A colleague was sentenced to prison.

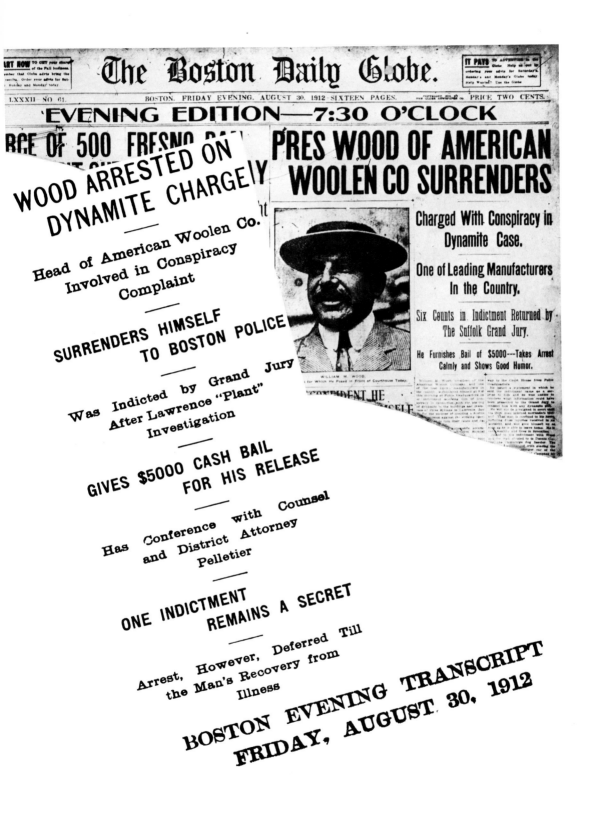

The Boston Daily Globe.

LXXXII NO 61.   BOSTON. FRIDAY EVENING. AUGUST 30. 1912-SIXTEEN PAGES.   PRICE TWO CENTS.

'EVENING EDITION—7:30 O'CLOCK

RGE OF 500 FRESNO

WOOD ARRESTED ON DYNAMITE CHARGE

Head of American Woolen Co.
Involved in Conspiracy
Complaint

SURRENDERS HIMSELF TO BOSTON POLICE

Was Indicted by Grand Jury
After Lawrence "Plant"
Investigation

GIVES $5000 CASH BAIL FOR HIS RELEASE

Has Conference with Counsel
and District Attorney
Pelletier

ONE INDICTMENT REMAINS A SECRET

Arrest, However, Deferred Till
the Man's Recovery from
Illness

PRES WOOD OF AMERICAN WOOLEN CO SURRENDERS

Charged With Conspiracy in Dynamite Case.

One of Leading Manufacturers In the Country.

Six Counts in Indictment Returned by The Suffolk Grand Jury.

He Furnishes Bail of $5000---Takes Arrest Calmly and Shows Good Humor.

WILLIAM M. WOOD.

CONFIDENT HE

BOSTON EVENING TRANSCRIPT
FRIDAY, AUGUST 30, 1912

The support for Ettor and Giovannitti which was being demonstrated not only throughout America but also in many parts of the world had its effect.

So did the actions of working people in many industrial centers in staging walkouts and stoppages of work. And the indictment of Wood proved a stunning blow to the prosecution.

The jury deliberated five hours and came to its conclusion.

On November 23 Ettor, Giovannitti and Caruso were found *NOT GUILTY!*

TUESDAY, NOVEMBER 26,

ALL THREE
FOUND
NOT GUILTY

Two days later, on Thanksgiving Day, the working people of Lawrence welcomed Ettor and Giovannitti back with them, free men. Ettor spoke for two and one-half hours as 5,000 men, women and children stood silent.

"We owe our lives not to the laws of Massachusetts nor to the tricks of lawyers, but to the working class of America and the world," stated Ettor.

236

The words spoken by Giovannitti and Ettor during their trial ring as true today as they did in 1912:

"I learned at my mother's knee," Giovannitti told the court, *"to revere the name of a republic. . . . I ask the District Attorney, who speaks about the New England tradition, what he means by that—if he means the New England traditions of this same town where they used to burn the witches at the stake, or if he means the New England traditions of those men who refused to be any longer under the iron heel of the British authority and dumped the tea into Boston Harbor."*

Said Ettor: *"Does the District Attorney believe that . . . the gallows or the guillotine ever settled an idea? If an idea can live, it lives because history adjudges it right.*

"I only ask for justice. . . . The scaffold has never yet and never will destroy an idea or a movement. . . . An idea constituting a social crime in one age becomes the very religion of humanity in the next. . . . Whatever my social views are, they are what they are. They cannot be tried in this courtroom."

Photo research and book design by Rachel Cowan and Margot Jones.

The following photographs or paintings may not be from Lawrence, Massachusettes, but are in keeping with the spirit of the text: